D1075070

REDUCE, REUSE, RECYCLE!
CARING FOR OUR PLANET

By VITA JIMÉNEZ
Illustrations by GEORGE ERMOS
Music by MARK OBLINGER

CANTATA
LEARNING

WWW.CANTATALEARNING.COM

CANTATA
LEARNING

Published by Cantata Learning
1710 Roe Crest Drive
North Mankato, MN 56003
www.cantatalearning.com

A note to educators and librarians from the publisher: Cantata Learning has provided the following data to assist in book processing and suggested use of Cantata Learning product.

Publisher's Cataloging-in-Publication Data
Prepared by Librarian Consultant: Ann-Marie Begnaud
Library of Congress Control Number: 2016938065
    Reduce, Reuse, Recycle! : Caring for Our Planet
    Series: Me, My Friends, My Community : Caring for Our Planet
    By Vita Jiménez
    Illustrations by George Ermos
    Music by Mark Oblinger
    Summary: In this catchy song paired with colorful illustrations, children learn how to reduce, reuse, and recycle.
    ISBN: 978-1-63290-784-4 (library binding/CD)
Suggested Dewey and Subject Headings:
    Dewey: E 363.7282
    LCSH Subject Headings: Recycling (Waste, etc.) – Juvenile literature. | Environmental responsibility – Juvenile literature. | Recycling (Waste, etc.) – Songs and music – Texts. | Environmental responsibility – Songs and music – Texts. | Recycling (Waste, etc.) – Juvenile sound recordings. | Environmental responsibility – Juvenile sound recordings.
    Sears Subject Headings: Recycling. | Environmental protection. | School songbooks. | Children's songs. | World music.
    BISAC Subject Headings: JUVENILE NONFICTION / Recycling & Green Living. | JUVENILE NONFICTION / Music / Songbooks. | JUVENILE NONFICTION / Science & Nature / Environmental Conservation & Protection.

Book design and art direction: Tim Palin Creative
Editorial direction: Flat Sole Studio
Music direction: Elizabeth Draper
Music written and produced by Mark Oblinger

Printed in the United States of America in North Mankato, Minnesota.
122016   0339CGS17

ACCESS THE MUSIC!
SCAN CODE WITH MOBILE APP
CANTATALEARNING.COM

TIPS TO SUPPORT LITERACY AT HOME

WHY READING AND SINGING WITH YOUR CHILD IS SO IMPORTANT

Daily reading with your child leads to increased academic achievement. Music and songs, specifically rhyming songs, are a fun and easy way to build early literacy and language development. Music skills correlate significantly with both phonological awareness and reading development. Singing helps build vocabulary and speech development. And reading and appreciating music together is a wonderful way to strengthen your relationship.

READ AND SING EVERY DAY!

TIPS FOR USING CANTATA LEARNING BOOKS AND SONGS DURING YOUR DAILY STORY TIME

1. As you sing and read, point out the different words on the page that rhyme. Suggest other words that rhyme.

2. Memorize simple rhymes such as Itsy Bitsy Spider and sing them together. This encourages comprehension skills and early literacy skills.

3. Use the questions in the back of each book to guide your singing and storytelling.

4. Read the included sheet music with your child while you listen to the song. How do the music notes correlate to the words of the song?

5. Sing along on the go and at home. Access music by scanning the QR code on each Cantata book, or by using the included CD. You can also stream or download the music for free to your computer, smartphone, or mobile device.

Devoting time to daily reading shows that you are available for your child. Together, you are building language, literacy, and listening skills.

Have fun reading and singing!

Every day we throw things away. But what happens to all of that garbage? It usually ends up in a **landfill**. The **trash** can also create pollution that is harmful to the land, water, and air. But we can help to keep the Earth clean and green by learning to **reduce**, **reuse**, and **recycle**.

To learn how, turn the page and sing along!

Reduce! Reuse! Recycle!

Let's reduce!

When we leave a room,
we turn off all the lights.

Remember to turn off
what we don't use at night!

When we brush our teeth,
don't let the water run.

We turn off the faucet
as soon as we are done.

We make a lot of trash
each and every day.

We make a lot of trash,
but should we throw it all away?

There are things we can do
to help Earth each day.

Reduce, reuse, recycle!
We can do this right away!

TRASH

RECYCLE

COMPOST

Reduce! Reuse! Recycle!

Let's reuse!

Everyone can **donate**
their used clothes and shoes.

Don't throw them away.
They are things others can use!

13

After you're done drawing,
flip over the page.

You'll use less paper.
And there's a tree
    you might save!

We make a lot of trash
each and every day.

We make a lot of trash,
but should we throw it all away?

There are things we can do
to help Earth each day.

Reduce, reuse, recycle!
We can do this right away!

Reduce! Reuse! Recycle!

Let's recycle!

Glass, plastic, and paper,
no need to throw them away.

They can be recycled
and used again some day!

We make a lot of trash
each and every day.

We make a lot of trash,
but should we throw it all away?

There are things we can do
to help Earth each day.

Reduce, reuse, recycle!
We can do this right away!

Reduce, reuse, recycle!
Reduce, reuse, recycle!

SONG LYRICS
Reduce, Reuse, Recycle!

Reduce! Reuse! Recycle!
Let's reduce!

When we leave a room,
we turn off all the lights.
Remember to turn off
what we don't use at night!

When we brush our teeth,
don't let the water run.
We turn off the faucet
as soon as we are done.

We make a lot of trash
each and every day.
We make a lot of trash,
but should we throw it all away?

There are things we can do
to help Earth each day.
Reduce, reuse, recycle!
We can do this right away!

Reduce! Reuse! Recycle!
Let's reuse!

Everyone can donate
their used clothes and shoes.
Don't throw them away.
They are things others can use!

After you're done drawing,
flip over the page.
You'll use less paper.
And there's a tree you might save!

We make a lot of trash
each and every day.
We make a lot of trash,
but should we throw it all away?

There are things we can do
to help Earth each day.
Reduce, reuse, recycle!
We can do this right away!

Reduce! Reuse! Recycle!
Let's recycle!

Glass, plastic, and paper,
no need to throw them away.
They can be recycled
and used again some day!

We make a lot of trash
each and every day.
We make a lot of trash,
but should we throw it all away?

There are things we can do
to help Earth each day.
Reduce, reuse, recycle!
We can do this right away!

Reduce, reuse, recycle!
Reduce, reuse, recycle!

Reduce, Reuse, Recycle!

World
Mark Oblinger

Intro/Interlude

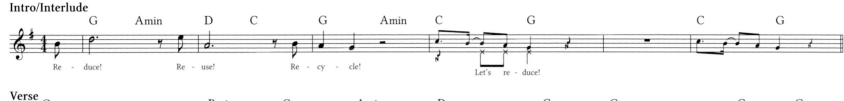

Re - duce! Re - use! Re - cy - cle! Let's re - duce!

Verse

1. When we leave a room, we turn off all the lights. Re - mem - ber to turn off what we don't use at night!

Verse 2
When we brush our teeth,
don't let the water run.
We turn off the faucet
as soon as we are done.

Chorus

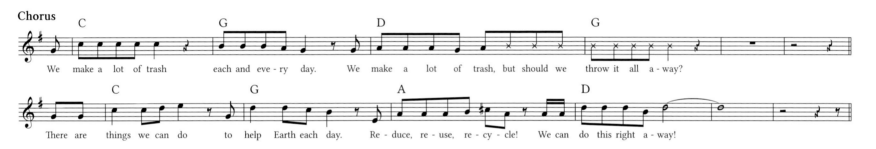

We make a lot of trash each and eve - ry day. We make a lot of trash, but should we throw it all a - way?

There are things we can do to help Earth each day. Re - duce, re - use, re - cy - cle! We can do this right a - way!

Interlude
Reduce! Reuse! Recycle!
Let's reuse!

Verse 3
Everyone can donate
their used clothes and shoes.
Don't throw them away.
They are things others can use!

Verse 4
After you're done drawing,
flip over the page.
You'll use less paper.
And there's a tree you might save!

Chorus

Interlude
Reduce! Reuse! Recycle!
Let's recycle!

Verse 5
Glass, plastic, and paper,
no need to throw them away.
They can be recycled
and used again some day!

Chorus

Outro

Re - duce! Re - use! Re - cy - cle!

23

GLOSSARY

donate—to give away

landfill—a place to bury garbage

recycle—to take old items and use them to make new ones

reduce—to use less of something

reuse—to use again

trash—things that have been thrown away

GUIDED READING ACTIVITIES

1. Why do you think the author wrote this book?

2. What did you learn about reducing, reusing, and recycling that you didn't know before?

3. If you had to explain recycling to a friend, what would you say?

4. What other things that you use can you reduce or reuse?

5. How do the illustrations help you to understand the text?

TO LEARN MORE

Ghigna, Charles. *Recycling Is Fun*. North Mankato, MN: Capstone, 2012.

Lepetit, Angie. *Trash Magic: A Book about Recycling a Plastic Bottle*. North Mankato, MN: Capstone, 2013.

Miller, Edward. *Recycling Day*. New York: Holiday House, 2014.

Weber, Rebecca. *Time to Recycle*. North Mankato, MN: Capstone, 2012.